Facts About the Raccoon Dog

By Lisa Strattin

© 2016 Lisa Strattin

Revised © 2019

Facts for Kids Picture Books by Lisa Strattin

Harlequin Macaw, Vol 34

Downy Woodpecker, Vol 37

Frilled Lizard, Vol 39

Purple Finch, Vol 48

Poison Dart Frogs, Vol 50

Giant Otter, Vol 57

Hornbill, Vol 67

Dwarf Lemur, Vol 73

Giant Squirrel, Vol 76

Star Tortoise, Vol 79

Sign Up for New Release Emails Here

http://LisaStrattin.com/subscribe-here

Monthly Surprise Box

http://KidCraftsByLisa.com

Contents

INTRODUCTION

The raccoon dog may look like the raccoon but it actually belongs to the dog family. However, some of its personality traits are similar to that of the raccoon. It is often seen as a pest. It can also climb trees similarly to the raccoon.

There are six different subspecies, or varieties, of the raccoon dog. It is not a concern to become an endangered species currently. Although, its population has started to decline in recent years.

CHARACTERISTICS

Often mistaken as a raccoon relative, this animal is actually a dog. However, it is nocturnal and most active at night when it searches for food. It is an omnivore like most dogs. It is seen as a pest as it has been known to hurt crops and livestock.

Sometimes, the raccoon dogs will play dead, like the possum, to fool its predators. They like to search for food in pairs, leaving the den and even pups alone together. These pairs are permanent and will last until one of them dies. Only then, will they find a new partner.

These pairs may also live in small groups with other couples, forming a pack. In addition, these couples will hibernate together and even groom each other. This is uncommon among other adult, domesticated or wild, dogs.

APPEARANCE

The raccoon dog looks a lot like the raccoon of North America, although it is not actually related to it. The raccoon dog has brownish fur or sometimes more gray with black bands like the raccoon's mask around its eyes. They also have a black strip across their backs. Their tails are dark in color, while their bellies are light.

During the summer months their fur can brighten to look reddish. They have whiskers on their faces and shorter wide ears that stand up. They have short legs and bushy tails. Their bodies are typically longer then the raccoon and appear slender.

LIFE STAGES

While the mother is pregnant, the father will bring her food. Babies, called pups, are born just after two months in the womb, usually early in Spring. Pups may have around five or six brothers and sisters. However, as many as a litter of sixteen happens occasionally.

Pups are born with their eyes closed and will open them when they are about one-week-old. Next, their teeth will come in and their hair gets lighter, leaving only the dark band surrounding their eyes. These pups will nurse from their mom for up to two months.

The father will help raise them and even babysit during the day. This allows the mother to leave and go look for food. Pups are considered full grown at just four and half months. By Autumn, the pups will leave their parents and find mates of their own. After a few more months, just under a year old, they will begin to become parents themselves.

LIFE SPAN

Although, the average life span of a raccoon dog is not exactly known, it is generally thought to live six or seven years in the wild. They have been known to live up to eleven years in captivity in zoos.

SIZE

Raccoon dogs range from 18 inches to 24 inches long, weighing on average around twenty pounds. They usually stand about nine inches tall when on all fours. Although this weight changes with the seasons, like their fur does, and they usually weigh less during spring months after coming out of hibernation.

HABITAT

The raccoon dog is native to Eastern Asia. It has since been introduced to Western Europe as well. However, it is viewed as a pest there.

The raccoon dog is the only in its family to hibernate during the winter months. During this hibernation it will remain in or very close to its den to conserve energy. It is also the only member of the dog family to climb trees other than the gray fox found in North America.

DIET

Raccoon dogs are omnivores and eat a variety of things from insects to birds, fish, rodents, and reptiles. They also enjoy corn, fruit, and berries as well. Some of their favorite fruit include watermelons and pears. They are true omnivores with a fairly balanced diet of both meats and plants.

Like their fur and weight, their diet changes seasonally. They tend to eat more fruit and frogs in the spring, switching to a fatty diet as winter nears. This will help give them the stored fat they need to survive the winter while hibernating. Birds make up to almost half of their diet.

FRIENDS AND ENEMIES

The largest threat to the raccoon dog is the wolf. It preys on up to half of the population of raccoon dogs! Eagles, large hawks, and large owls also hunt them. Since they are in competition for the same food, the fox and badger may also hurt them.

Raccoon dogs are not aggressive and will often flee when threatened. These animals are also hunted for their pelts, or fur, and to protect game birds, crops and livestock. Hunting season is usually between late fall and early winter, just before they hibernate to avoid the deeper snow.

Their bones are also used in ancient Eastern medicines in countries like China. They are friends with other couples and live near other raccoon dogs.

SUITABILITY AS PETS

Raccoon dogs would not make very good pets mainly because of the numerous diseases and parasites they often carry, including rabies. This would be dangerous for you and your family. They are also nocturnal and would want to play at night not during the day like you.

Being meat eaters they also have sharp claws and teeth as well. They have not been domesticated and would not do tricks like most household dogs. They would not "sit", "rollover", or 'shake". But, they would "play dead," since this is part of their nature. If handled from birth, they remain friendly. But for now, it is best to choose a dog breed that has already been tamed as a family pet.

COLOR ME

COLOR ME

COLOR ME

COLOR ME

Please leave me a review here:

http://lisastrattin.com/Review-Vol-161

For more Kindle Downloads Visit Lisa Strattin Author Page on Amazon Author Central

http://amazon.com/author/lisastrattin

To see upcoming titles, visit my website at LisaStrattin.com– all books available on kindle!

http://lisastrattin.com

RACCOON DOG PRINT

You can get one by copying and pasting this link into your browser:

http://lisastrattin.com/RaccoonDogPrint

MONTHLY SURPRISE BOX

Get yours by copying and pasting this link into your browser

http://KidCraftsByLisa.com

Made in the USA
Middletown, DE
27 January 2022

59848642R00022